CONTENTS

WHAT ARE BONES?

Press your forehead or pinch your finger, and you'll feel something rock-hard inside – your bones! You don't normally see them, but bones are an essential body part, not just for us humans, but for many other animals too, from cats and dogs to birds, whales and frogs. Bones support the body, protect soft organs like the brain, and do other jobs as well.

Bones contain a lot of the mineral calcium, making them strong and stiff. But they are still living body parts, with blood flowing through them.

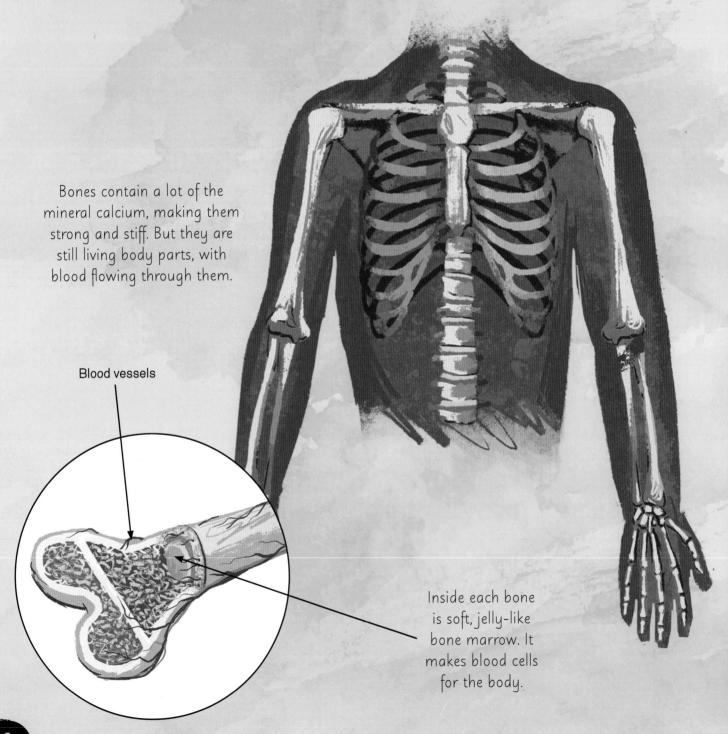

Blood vessels

Inside each bone is soft, jelly-like bone marrow. It makes blood cells for the body.

T BOOK OF

MAL
IES

BY ANNA CLAYBOURNE

WAYLAND
www.waylandbooks.co.uk

First published in Great Britain in 2020 by Wayland
Copyright © Hodder and Stoughton, 2020

Managing Editor: Victoria Brooker
Design and artwork: Collaborate

**Produced with the assistance of experts
at the Natural History Museum, London**

ISBN: 978 1 5263 1246 4 (hbk)
ISBN: 978 1 5263 1247 1 (pbk)

10 9 8 7 6 5 4 3 2 1

Wayland, an imprint of
Hachette Children's Group
Part of Hodder and Stoughton
Carmelite House
50 Victoria Embankment
London EC4Y 0DZ
An Hachette UK Company
www.hachette.co.uk
www.hachettechildrens.co.uk

Printed and bound in China

The website addresses (URLs) included in this book
were valid at the time of going to press. However, it is
possible that contents or addresses may have changed
since the publication of this book.No responsibility for
any such changes can be accepted by either the author
or the Publisher.

Bones are made up of several layers.

Spongy bone looks like a sponge (but it's hard, not squishy)

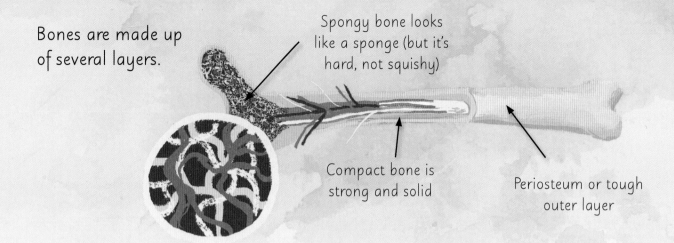

Compact bone is strong and solid

Periosteum or tough outer layer

ANIMALS WITH BONES

There are five groups of vertebrates – the scientific name for animals with bones.

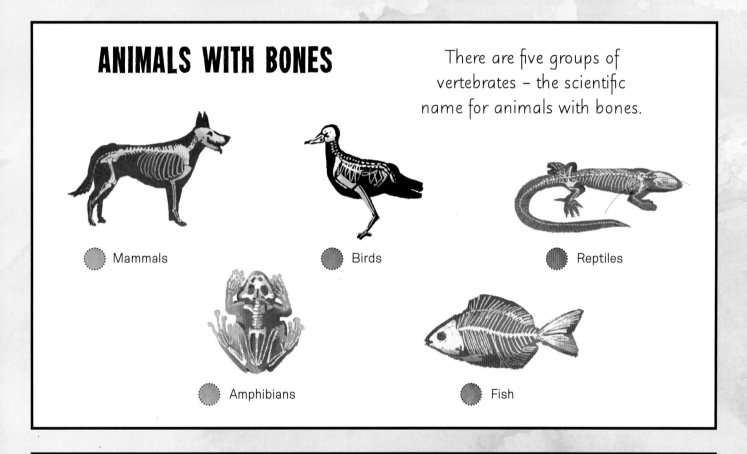

Mammals

Birds

Reptiles

Amphibians

Fish

ANIMALS WITHOUT BONES

If all these animals need bones, why doesn't a worm or an octopus? Animals with no bones are called invertebrates. They are usually small, so they don't have big bodies to hold up. Or, like a giant octopus, they live in water, which helps to support their weight.

Hard outer shell, or exoskeleton

Beetle

Giant Pacific octopus

ANIMAL SKELETONS

Did you know you have over 200 different bones? Bones don't work on their own – instead, lots of bones join together to make a skeleton. Animal skeletons come in many shapes and sizes. They can include legs, arms, wings or flippers. Some have tails, while others don't. But if you look closely, you'll see that all skeletons have the same basic layout and main parts.

Spider monkey   Flamingo   Kangaroo   Human

All vertebrate animals have a skull. It surrounds and protects the soft, jelly-like brain, and also holds important bits like eyes, ears, jaws and teeth.

The spine, or backbone, is a row of knobbly bones down the middle of the back, linking the rest of the skeleton together.

Human spine   Fish spine

Flamingo   Lizard   Human

Frogs and toads don't have tails.

In most animals, the spine continues into a tail.

HOW MANY LIMBS?

A typical skeleton has four limbs, but a few have lost their limbs – like snakes, for example.

MOVING PARTS

Bones are linked by flexible joints, allowing the skeleton to move. Muscles are attached to bones by tendons and pull on them to make them change position.

Elbow joint

Muscle

BONY BITS

More than half of your bones are in your hands and feet!

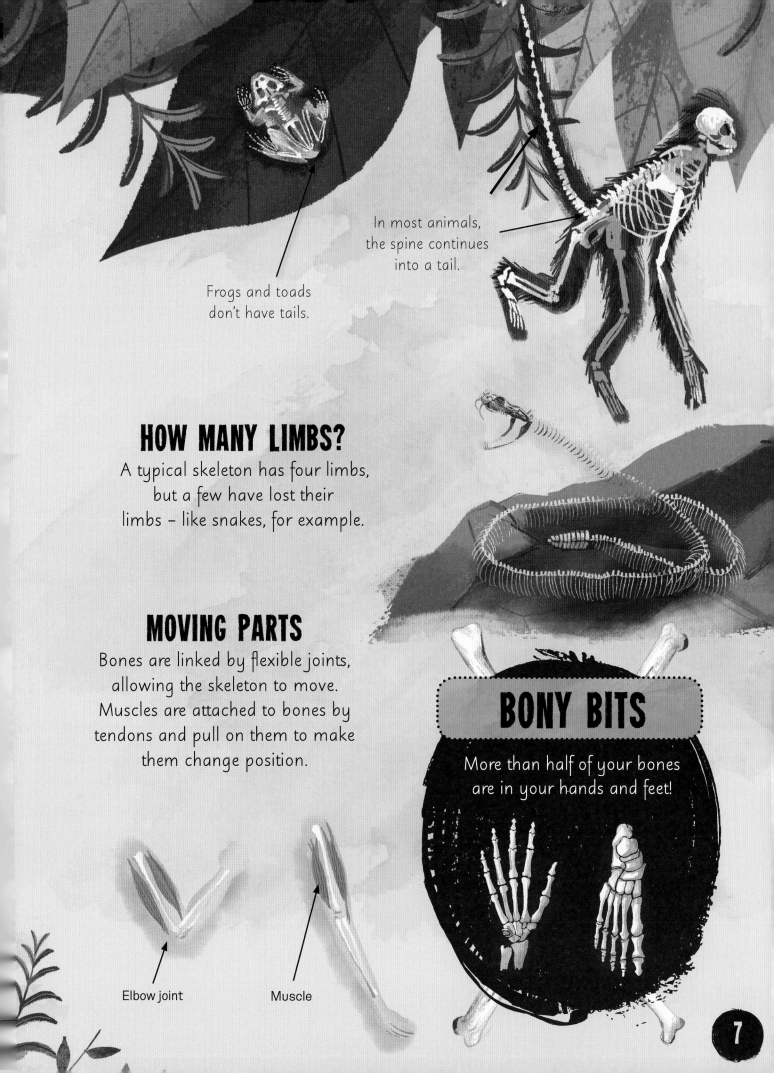

RACCOON

The raccoon belongs to the mammal family of vertebrates. Mammals feed their babies on milk, and usually have hair or fur. Like many mammals, raccoons are furry, with four legs and a tail. Raccoons are omnivores, meaning they eat all types of food, and they're often spotted in cities looking for leftovers. They are also very clever, and brilliant at using their front paws like hands.

RACCOON PAWS

Raccoons often use both paws together to hold food.

As in many other animals, you can see the same basic parts in a raccoon's skeleton as in a human's.

Thigh bone or femur

Heel bone

Knee

Toe bones or phalanges

BONE TOOLS

Archaeologists have found prehistoric tools made from raccoon bones, including fish hooks and needles.

Skull

Big eye sockets

Raccoons have big eyes, as they are mostly nocturnal and look for food at night.

RACCOON TEETH

An animal's teeth can reveal clues about what it eats. Raccoons have sharp front teeth for eating meat and fish, and wider back teeth for chewing plants.

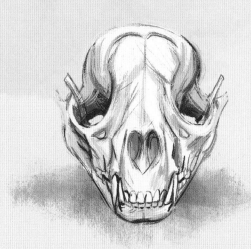

Like humans, raccoons have five long finger bones in their paws. Unlike humans, they don't have thumbs, but they can still hold things in their 'hands'.

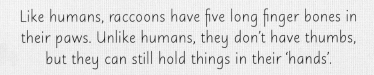

GIRAFFE

Giraffes are famous for being tall – VERY tall. A giraffe can reach 6 m (20 ft) in height, making it the tallest land animal in the world. Being tall helps the giraffe to reach tree leaves, its favourite food, and to spot predators from a distance.

The giraffe's neck isn't just long, it's thick and heavy too. Each neck bone can be up to 25 cm (10 in) across, the size of a football!

Giraffes have long, skinny leg bones. The bones that form hands and feet in humans are fused together and stretched, adding extra length.

'Wrist'

'Hand' bones

GIRAFFE HORNS

Giraffes have two short, knobbly bone horns, called 'ossicones'. They are part of the giraffe's skull and, unlike most animal horns, they're covered with skin and fur.

Ossicones

Male giraffes use their necks, heads and ossicones to whack each other in fights.

SHORT NECKS

Even mammals that seem to have no necks, like this hamster, have seven neck bones.

NECK BONES

You might think a giraffe's super-long neck would have extra neck bones, but it doesn't. In fact, giraffes have only seven neck bones – the same number as humans and most other mammals.

BAT

Bats are the only mammals that can truly fly, and their skeletons show how they do it. Unlike birds, bats don't have feathers. Instead, they have wings made of thin, leathery skin, stretched over long, skinny wing bones. Their other bones are as small and narrow as possible, to make their bodies light enough to fly.

A bat's wing bones are actually very long, light, spread-out finger bones, or phalanges.

The arm bones flap the wing, then fold it up like an umbrella when the bat isn't flying.

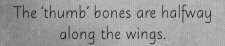

The 'thumb' bones are halfway along the wings.

Wing claw

They have hooked claws, which the bat uses to climb tree trunks or walls.

PTEROSAURS

Prehistoric flying reptiles called pterosaurs had similar wings to bats, with skin stretched over their arm bones.

HANGING ON

Bats are famous for hanging upside down to sleep, using their strong feet and talons. A bat's foot bones are linked to its body with long, stringy tendons. When the bat relaxes and lets its body drop down, the claws are pulled closed, so the bat can't fall off!

LITTLE LEGS

Bats can't stand or walk on their tiny legs. Instead, they crawl on all fours, using their wing claws too.

ELEPHANT

The elephant's best-known body part is its trunk. But take a closer look at its skeleton, and you'll see that the trunk is missing. That's because it evolved from the tip of the elephant's nose and its upper lip, and these body parts don't have bones. (Feel your own to check!)

Elephants are the world's biggest, heaviest land animals. If their leg bones were as thin as a human's, they would break under the weight. They have to be really thick to support the elephant's heavy body.

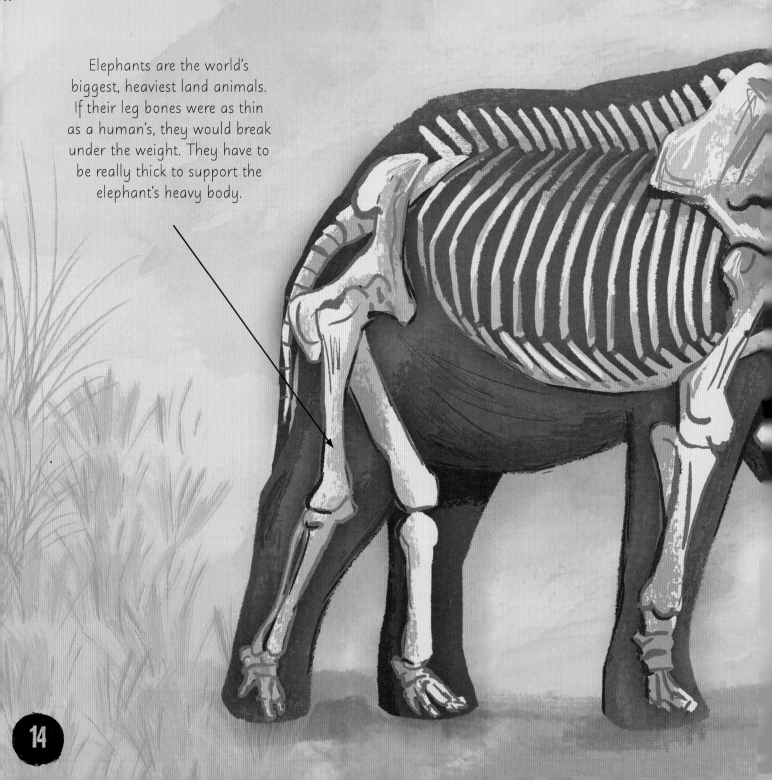

IVORY

Ivory is the hard, white substance elephant tusks are made from. It's been used for centuries to make ornaments, knife handles, piano keys and many other things – even false teeth for humans! Killing elephants for ivory is now banned, but it still happens.

An elephant's tusks are actually its extra-long front teeth. It uses them to fight off predators, dig up plants to eat, or show off to a mate.

TUSKS

A male African elephant's tusks can reach over 3 m (10 ft) long.

SKULL OF THE CYCLOPS

An elephant's skull has a large hole in the front where the trunk attaches. Some people think the myth of the Cyclops, a one-eyed giant, began when people found old elephant skulls and thought the hole was an enormous single eye socket.

GIBBON

Look at these incredible arms! This is a gibbon, a small member of the ape family, related to chimpanzees and gorillas. Its arm bones are MUCH longer than its leg bones. Gibbons live in jungles and get around by swinging between tree branches. Their extra-long arms allow them to reach further and swing across big gaps.

The gibbon's arm bones are almost the same length as the rest of its body.

Like other apes, gibbons have four fingers with a thumb opposite them, called an opposable thumb. This helps the hand to hold branches and other objects.

SPECIAL WRIST

The gibbon's wrist has a ball-and-socket joint, so its hands can move and turn more freely than a human's.

FAST ARMS

Thanks to their long arms, gibbons are the fastest ape. They can swing through the forest at up to 55 km/h (34 mph) – faster than the fastest human can run!

Brain cavity

Eye sockets

CLOSE COUSINS

Does this skull look familiar? Gibbons are close relatives of humans, as we are also members of the ape family. Their skulls are similar to ours, with forward-facing eye sockets and space for a large brain.

HUMAN

This is what the skeleton inside most people looks like. When we're born, we have over 270 bones, but by adulthood most people only have about 206. They don't disappear – it's just that some bones fuse together as you grow older, such as the bones that make up the skull.

Skull

Fused sections

As we don't need them for walking, our hands are free for holding, making and doing things.

Finger bones

Hand bones

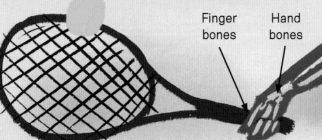

Spine

Unlike most other mammals, humans walk upright on two legs. This can cause backache, as the spine bones press down on each other.

Humans evolved from monkey-like animals with tails. Inside the body, the skeleton still has a tiny leftover tail, called the tailbone.

SMILE!

You can see part of your skeleton when you look in the mirror – your teeth! Teeth are not bones, but are attached to your jawbone.

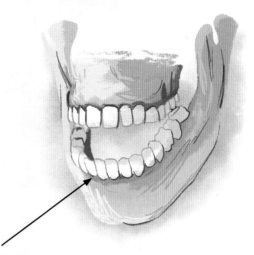

Teeth fit into sockets in your jawbones

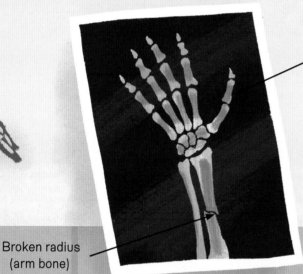

X-ray photo

Broken radius (arm bone)

BROKEN BONES

If a bone breaks, it will gradually build new bone and repair itself, but it has to be held still in the right position.

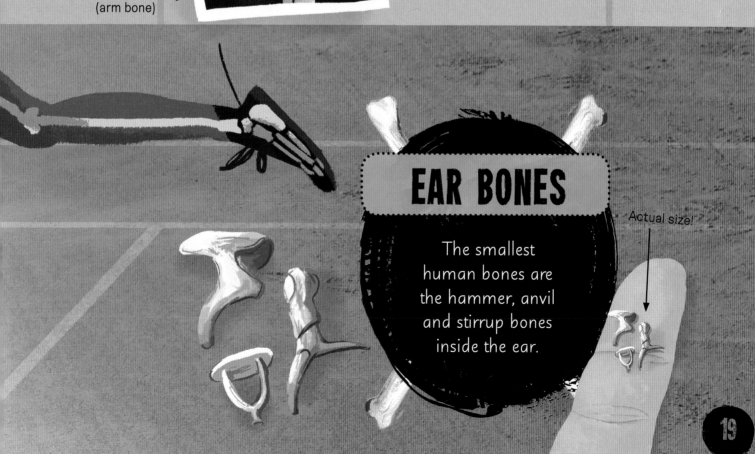

EAR BONES

Actual size!

The smallest human bones are the hammer, anvil and stirrup bones inside the ear.

BLUE WHALE

This is the skeleton of the world's biggest animal, the blue whale. Whales are mammals that have adapted to live in the sea. They evolved from furry, four-legged land animals that were only about the size of a large dog.

The skeleton can be up to 25 m (82 ft) long

Many whales have enormous heads. The blue whale's skull takes up over a quarter of the length of the skeleton.

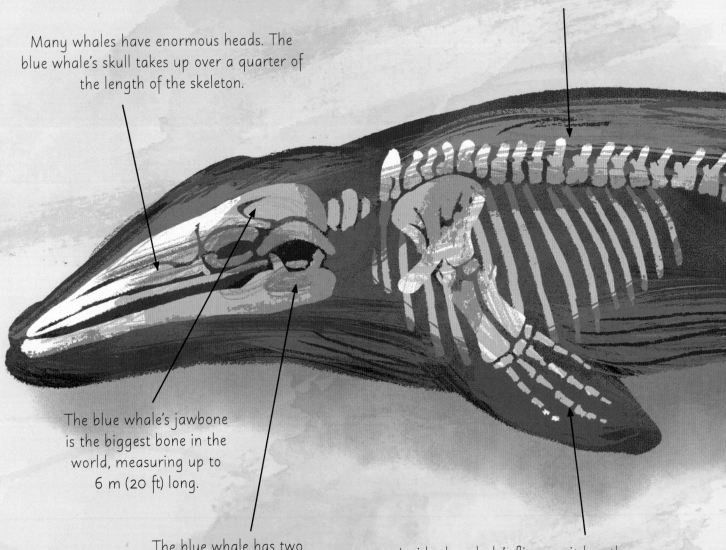

The blue whale's jawbone is the biggest bone in the world, measuring up to 6 m (20 ft) long.

The blue whale has two jawbones like this, one on each side.

Inside the whale's flippers, it has the same kind of finger bones found in humans, dogs and other mammals.

Jawbones

BIG MOUTH

Blue whales need big mouths, as they feed by gulping in a huge amount of water, then filtering food out of it. Blue whale jawbones are so big they were once used to make archways.

LEFTOVER LEGS

Over many generations, the whale's back legs shrank and disappeared. All that's left now are two small bones near the tail, just below the spine.

The blue whale's leftover leg bones

WANDERING ALBATROSS

These amazingly long wing bones belong to the wandering albatross, one of the biggest birds in the world, and one of the best fliers. It can glide for 1,000 km (600 miles) over the sea without even flapping its wings, and flies more than 100,000 km (600,000 miles) in a year.

Finger bones

Wrist

Unlike a bat, a bird's wing bones only run along the top or front of its wing.

Arm bones

Albatrosses have large beaks for grabbing food from the sea.

Birds' beaks are made of bone, with a hard covering similar to our fingernails.

The breastbone or sternum has a big, sticking-out blade or 'keel'. The large chest muscles that power the wings join onto it.

HOLLOW BONES

Flying birds have air spaces inside many of their bones. This helps them to collect extra oxygen, and also makes the bones light compared to their strength.

Extra-strong bone

Spaces inside

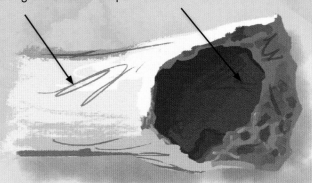

An albatross has a wingspan of up to 3.5 m (11.2 ft)

TUNEFUL BONES

New Zealand's Maori people traditionally used albatross wing bones to make flutes.

Short wings that flap very fast, instead of gliding

Sword-billed hummingbird

Long, thin beak for reaching into flowers

BIG AND SMALL

Birds come in a huge range of shapes and sizes – the smallest hummingbirds, for example, are only about 6cm (2.5 inches) long, as big as an albatross's toe bone.

BARN OWL

Owls' skeletons look quite unlike living owls! You can recognise an owl by its large head and wide, flat face, but this shape is created by its feathers. Inside, it has a much smaller, narrower skull. Owls also have much longer legs and necks than you might think.

An owl's eyeballs are tube-shaped, and held in place by rings of bone called sclerotic rings. This means owls can't move their eyes around – they can only look straight ahead.

Owls are nocturnal and hunt at night. Their huge eyes help them to see in dim light.

Owls hunt smaller animals like mice and voles. They have powerful beaks and long toes with sharp claws, for grabbing and tearing up prey.

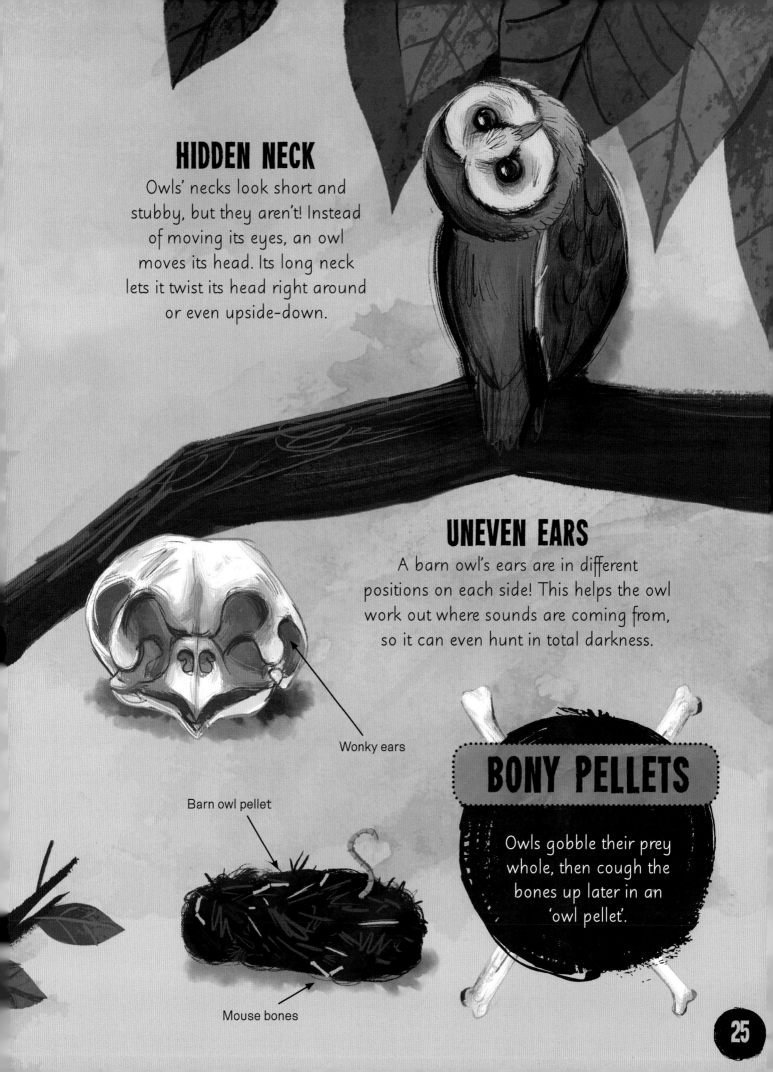

HIDDEN NECK

Owls' necks look short and stubby, but they aren't! Instead of moving its eyes, an owl moves its head. Its long neck lets it twist its head right around or even upside-down.

UNEVEN EARS

A barn owl's ears are in different positions on each side! This helps the owl work out where sounds are coming from, so it can even hunt in total darkness.

Wonky ears

BONY PELLETS

Owls gobble their prey whole, then cough the bones up later in an 'owl pellet'.

Barn owl pellet

Mouse bones

25

CASSOWARY

Not all birds can fly. Flightless birds, like emus, ostriches and cassowaries, have thicker, heavier bones than flying birds, and smaller wings, as they don't need to lift off into the air. They use their long, powerful legs for running and kicking.

The top of the cassowary's skull sticks up forming a bony crest or 'casque'.

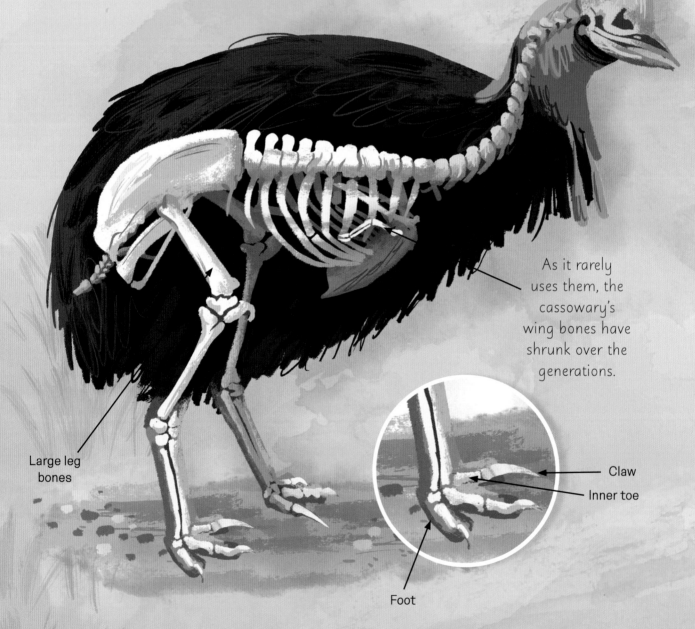

As it rarely uses them, the cassowary's wing bones have shrunk over the generations.

Large leg bones

Claw

Inner toe

Foot

The inner toe on each foot has an extra long, razor-sharp claw. Cassowaries use these to defend themselves.

Cassowary eggs are green, and up to 14 cm (5.5 in) long.

BONY EGGS

Birds lay eggs with hard shells containing the mineral calcium – the same mineral that makes bones hard and strong. If there isn't enough calcium in a bird's diet to make the shells, it uses calcium from its own skeleton.

MINI WINGS

Thanks to its kicking legs and killer claws, the cassowary is the most dangerous bird to humans – cassowaries have even been known to kill people.

WATER WINGS

Penguins are flightless birds that swim in the sea. Their wings have become flippers, which they use to 'fly' underwater.

Flipper bones

NILE CROCODILE

Don't mess with a Nile crocodile! This fierce, powerful hunter is instantly recognisable by its massive head and long, snapping jaws. Crocs live in and around rivers and swamps, and hunt any prey they can find, including humans. They are reptiles, and are related to alligators, lizards, snakes and turtles, as well as to the dinosaurs.

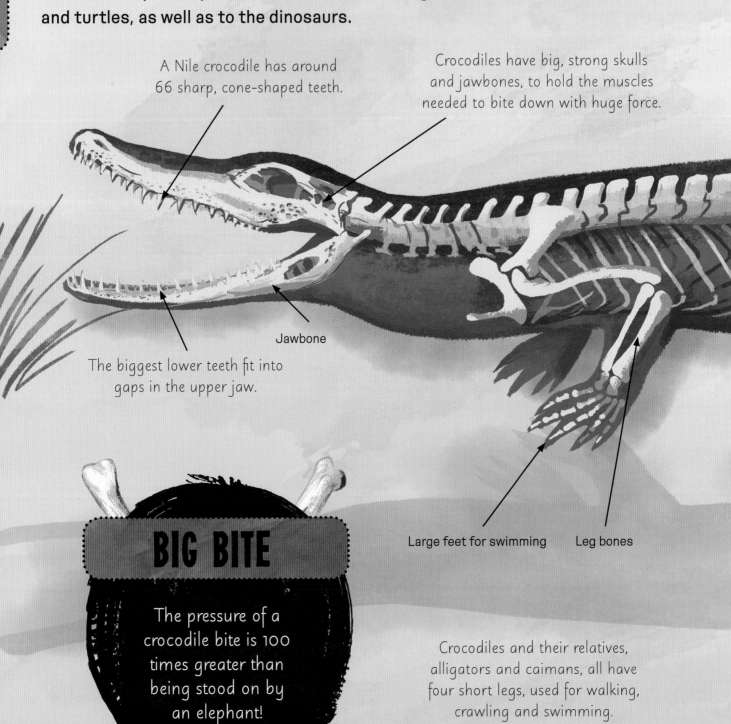

A Nile crocodile has around 66 sharp, cone-shaped teeth.

Crocodiles have big, strong skulls and jawbones, to hold the muscles needed to bite down with huge force.

Jawbone

The biggest lower teeth fit into gaps in the upper jaw.

Large feet for swimming

Leg bones

BIG BITE

The pressure of a crocodile bite is 100 times greater than being stood on by an elephant!

Crocodiles and their relatives, alligators and caimans, all have four short legs, used for walking, crawling and swimming.

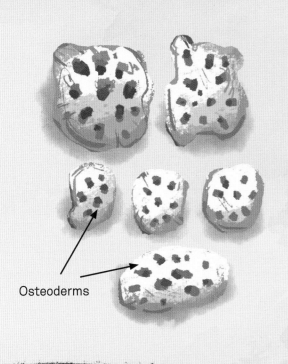

Osteoderms

SKIN BONES

Crocodiles and alligators have bones in their skin! Small, hard, plates of bone, called osteoderms, grow just under the skin to act as armour. They are not part of the main skeleton.

Crocodile: narrower, pointier skull

Alligator: wider, squarer skull

SPOT THE DIFFERENCE

Crocodiles and alligators are similar, but you can tell the difference by the shape of their skulls.

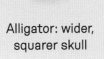

GREEN SEA TURTLE

Turtles and tortoises are different to most vertebrates, thanks to their hard, protective shells. Unlike a snail, a turtle doesn't just shelter inside its shell – the shell is part of its skeleton, and is connected to the bones inside its body.

The shell is made up of plates of bone that grow from the turtle's ribs and backbone.

A turtle also has a bony shell on its underside, called the plastron.

Turtles don't have teeth – they have sharp 'beaks' instead.

Finger bones

Flipper

Like many other animals with flippers, a turtle's flippers contain a hand-like skeleton.

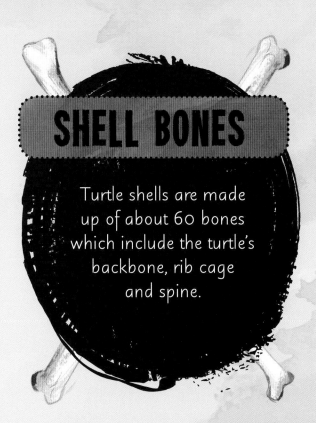

SHELL BONES

Turtle shells are made up of about 60 bones which include the turtle's backbone, rib cage and spine.

BEAUTIFUL SCUTES

When a sea turtle is alive, its bony shell is covered by patterned plates called scutes, made of a hard material similar to our fingernails. Some turtles, such as the hawksbill sea turtle, have been hunted for their scutes, which are known as 'tortoiseshell'.

Hawksbill sea turtle

Hawksbill 'tortoiseshell'

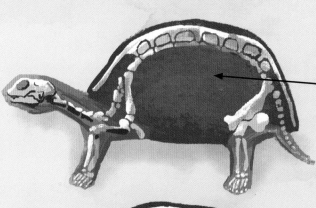

Turtle

HIDING INSIDE

Sea turtles cannot hide their heads inside their shells, but tortoises, their land-living relatives, can.

A tortoise bends its neck to pull it into the shell.

KING COBRA

Snakes, like this king cobra, are reptiles with no legs. Though they are very flexible and can curl up into coils, a snake is not soft and squishy like a worm. They're actually full of bones, including a skull, a spine, a tail and LOTS of ribs.

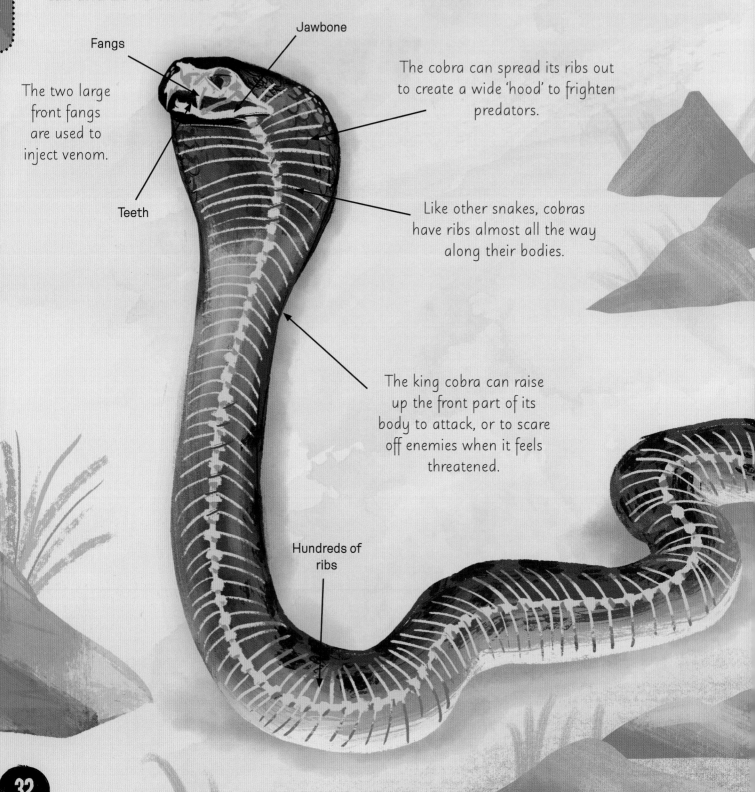

Jawbone

Fangs

The two large front fangs are used to inject venom.

Teeth

The cobra can spread its ribs out to create a wide 'hood' to frighten predators.

Like other snakes, cobras have ribs almost all the way along their bodies.

The king cobra can raise up the front part of its body to attack, or to scare off enemies when it feels threatened.

Hundreds of ribs

OPEN WIDE!

Snakes can swallow animals bigger than their own heads! Their skulls have special features to help them do this.

Lower jaw is separated, so it can spread out to wrap around prey.

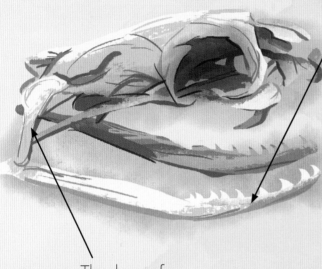

The shape of the jawbones lets the mouth open extra-wide.

TALL SNAKES

A king cobra can grow to 5.5 m (18 ft) long. When it rears up, its front part is as tall as a human!

MINI LEGS

Snakes evolved from lizards and some, like pythons, do actually have tiny leftover back leg bones.

Leg bones

BRACHIOSAURUS

Here are some of the best-known bones of all - dinosaur bones. Dinosaurs were a group of reptiles that lived more than 65 million years ago. We mostly know about them from their fossilised bones. This is Brachiosaurus, a huge, long-necked plant-eater. It was around 20 m (66 ft) long and 12 m (40 ft) tall.

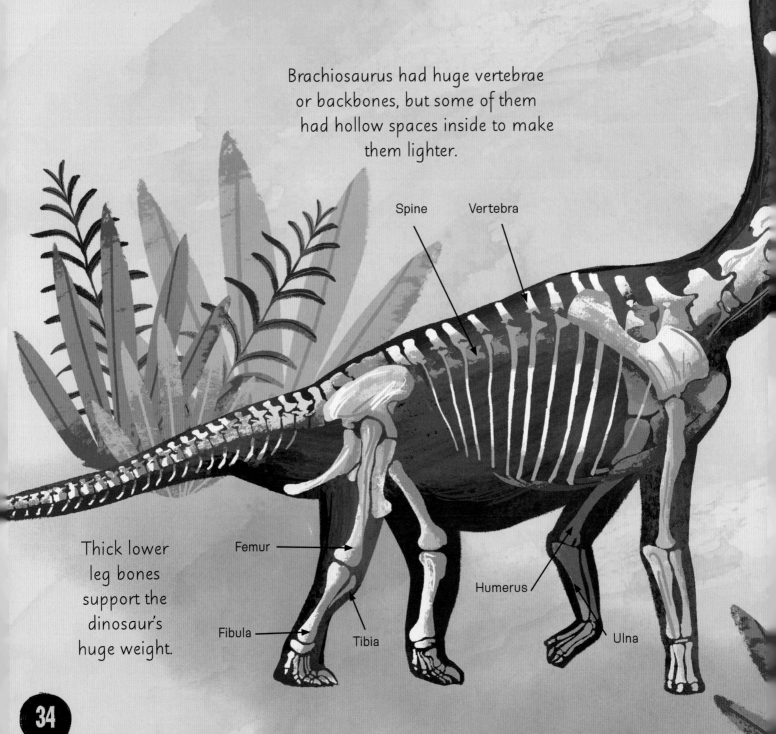

Brachiosaurus had huge vertebrae or backbones, but some of them had hollow spaces inside to make them lighter.

Spine

Vertebra

Thick lower leg bones support the dinosaur's huge weight.

Femur

Humerus

Fibula

Tibia

Ulna

The small skull has holes in it, making it lighter. They're called fenestrae (meaning 'windows').

DRAGON BONES

When people first found dinosaur bones, they thought they were from dragons or giants!

BIZARRE BONES

Some dinosaurs had very strange bones …

Long bone crest on skull

Parasaurolophus

Huge neck frill

Pentaceratops

Ankylosaurus

Huge bony lump on the end of the tail

COMMON FROG

Frogs, toads, newts and salamanders are amphibians, and most of them spend at least part of their lives in water. Frogs usually have thin, hollow bones, giving them strength and lightness for jumping. They also have fewer bones than most animals, with no ribs, tail or neck.

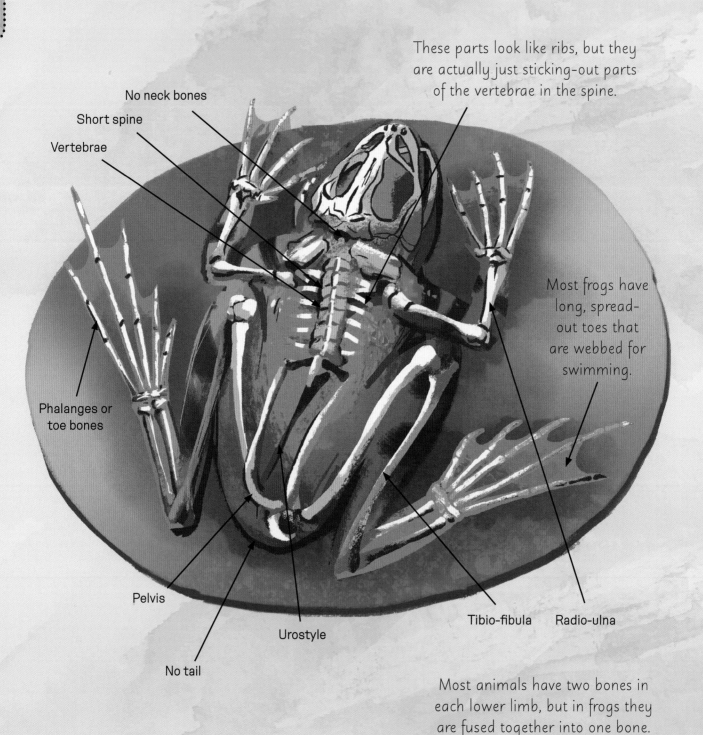

These parts look like ribs, but they are actually just sticking-out parts of the vertebrae in the spine.

No neck bones

Short spine

Vertebrae

Most frogs have long, spread-out toes that are webbed for swimming.

Phalanges or toe bones

Pelvis

Urostyle

No tail

Tibio-fibula   Radio-ulna

Most animals have two bones in each lower limb, but in frogs they are fused together into one bone.

Urostyle

BOING!!!

Most frogs have long back legs for jumping. They also have very long pelvis bones for their strong muscles to attach to. The bottom end of the spine is fused into a single bone called a urostyle, giving the back extra strength.

Actual size

TINY BONES

The smallest known skeleton of all belongs to a frog – a tiny tree frog from Papua New Guinea, only 7.7 mm long.

GREEN BONES

Glass frogs are small frogs with transparent skin, which means you can see the organs and bones inside their bodies. Some glass frogs have green bones!

Cochranella glass frog

37

GIANT SALAMANDER

Salamanders are amphibians, like frogs, but their body shape makes them look more like a lizard. The Chinese giant salamander is the biggest amphibian in the world, growing up to 1.8 m (6 feet) long – the size of a tall human!

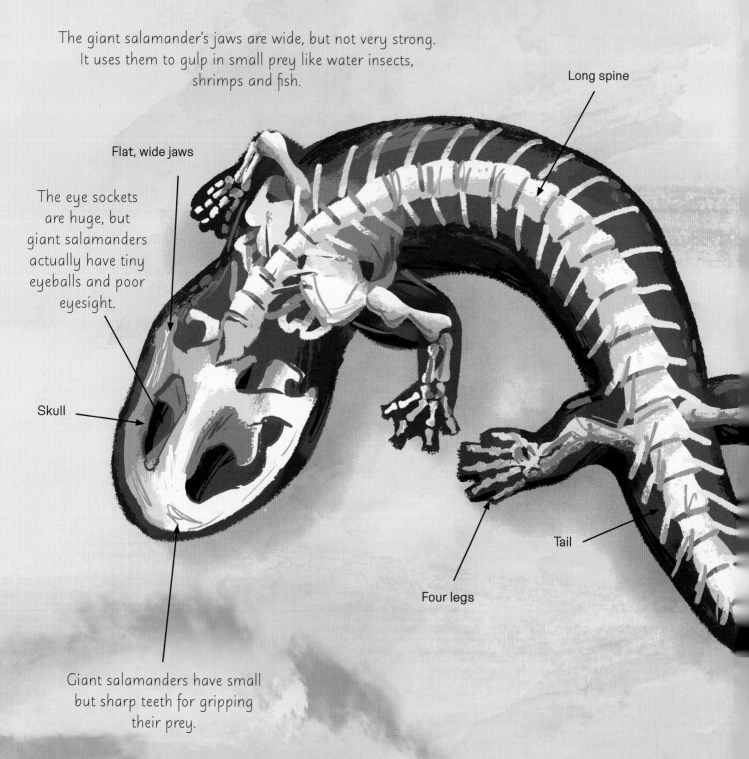

The giant salamander's jaws are wide, but not very strong. It uses them to gulp in small prey like water insects, shrimps and fish.

Long spine

Flat, wide jaws

The eye sockets are huge, but giant salamanders actually have tiny eyeballs and poor eyesight.

Skull

Four legs

Tail

Giant salamanders have small but sharp teeth for gripping their prey.

JUST GROW A NEW ONE!

Some species of salamander have an amazing ability. If they lose their tail or a leg, they can grow themselves a new one, including growing brand-new bones.

Amputated leg →

New cells →

New bone and skin →

Regrown leg →

RIPPING RIBS

An amphibian called the Iberian ribbed newt has rib bones with sharp tips like claws. If a predator grabs the newt, it can push the sharp rib tips right out through its skin to stab the predator's mouth.

Iberian ribbed newt →

LONGNOSE BUTTERFLYFISH

It's easy to see how this fish got its name! Its long nose, or snout, is part of its skull and is made of bone. Butterflyfish, which usually live on coral reefs, belong to the bony fish family, the most common type of fish. Their skeletons are made of hard bone (unlike the fish on the next page!).

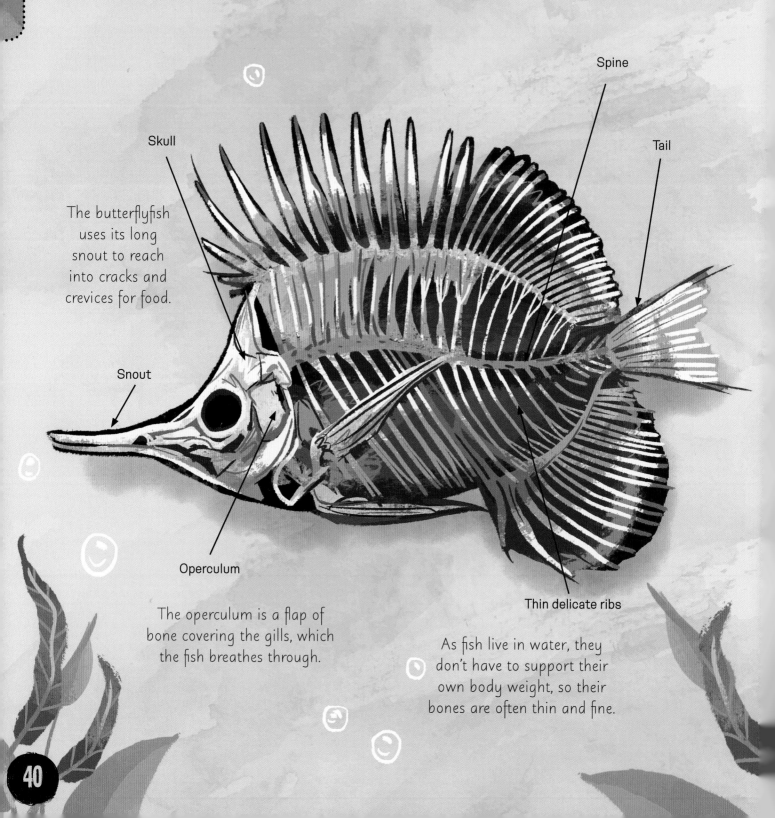

Spine

Skull

Tail

The butterflyfish uses its long snout to reach into cracks and crevices for food.

Snout

Operculum

The operculum is a flap of bone covering the gills, which the fish breathes through.

Thin delicate ribs

As fish live in water, they don't have to support their own body weight, so their bones are often thin and fine.

FISH FINS

In most fish, the thin fin bones are dermal bones, meaning they grow in the skin, and are not connected to the main skeleton.

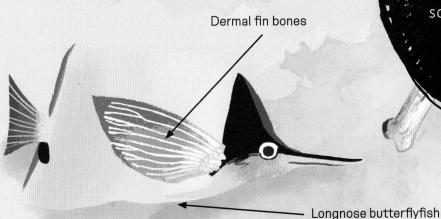

Dermal fin bones

Longnose butterflyfish

EAR BONES

Instead of eardrums like us, fish sense sound vibrations using bones in their ears, called otoliths.

MORE BONY FISH

Bony fish come in a huge range of shapes and sizes, as these skeletons show:

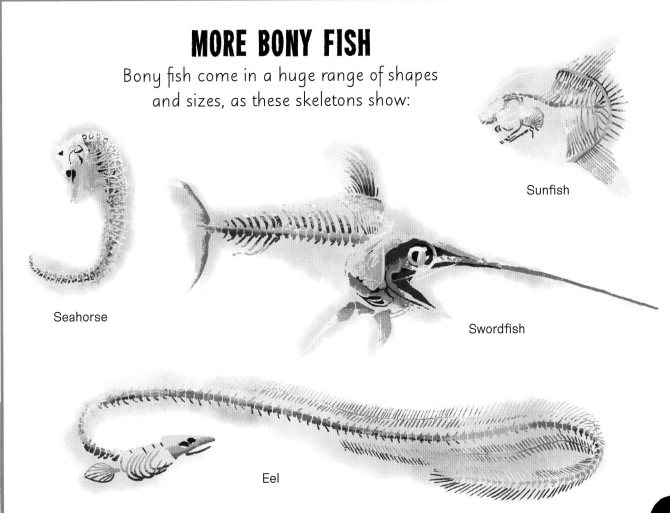

Sunfish

Seahorse

Swordfish

Eel

HAMMERHEAD SHARK

This strange-looking shark shouldn't really be in this book at all. Why? Because it doesn't have any bones! Sharks do have skeletons, but they are made from soft, rubbery cartilage instead of bone. Because of this, sharks are called cartilaginous fish.

Cartilage is similar to bone, but contains less calcium. It's light and flexible, allowing the shark to twist and turn its body.

The shark's wide head looks like a hammer from above. The shark sweeps it from side to side to scan the seabed for prey.

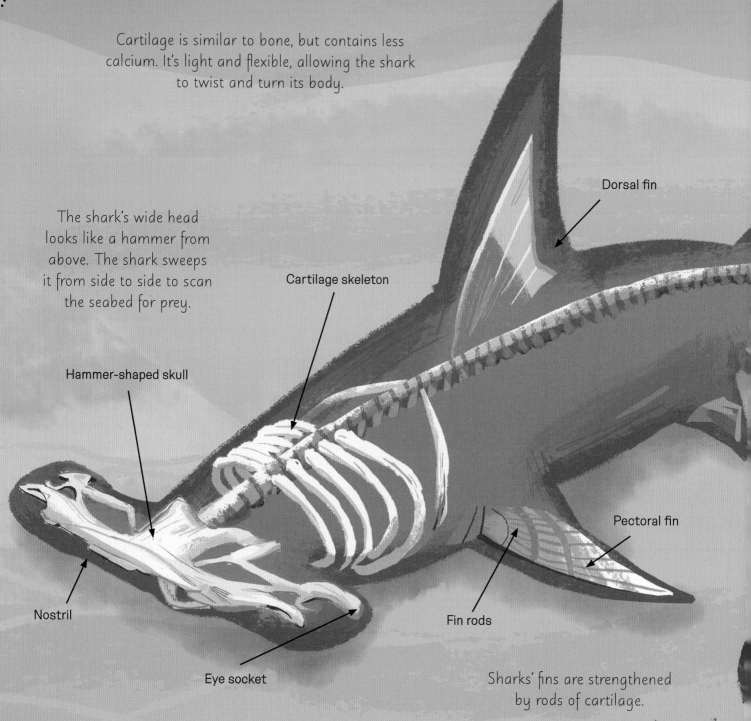

Dorsal fin

Cartilage skeleton

Hammer-shaped skull

Pectoral fin

Nostril

Fin rods

Eye socket

Sharks' fins are strengthened by rods of cartilage.

SHARK TEETH

Shark teeth are harder than the rest of a shark's skeleton. They are arranged in rows that gradually move forward in the shark's mouth. When the row at the front wears out, another replaces it.

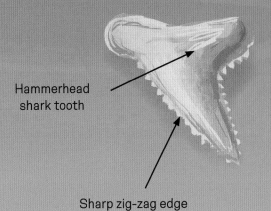

Hammerhead shark tooth

Sharp zig-zag edge

BENDY BITS

We have cartilage in our ears and noses. That's why they feel bendy!

RAYS

Rays are sharks' closest relatives, and also belong to the cartilaginous fish family. Instead of fins, they have wide 'wings' which they ripple to swim through the water.

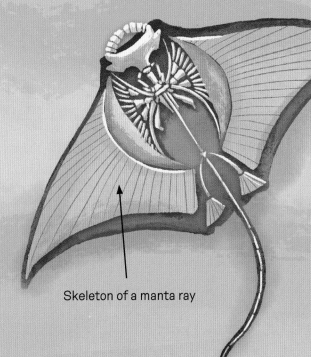

Skeleton of a manta ray

BONES LEFT BEHIND

Bones are partly made of minerals, which do not rot away. After an animal dies, the rest of its body decays quite fast, but its bones last for much longer. Sometimes, bones are buried by mud or sand that slowly hardens into rock, becoming fossilised. By digging up fossils from prehistoric times, we can find out about things that lived long ago.

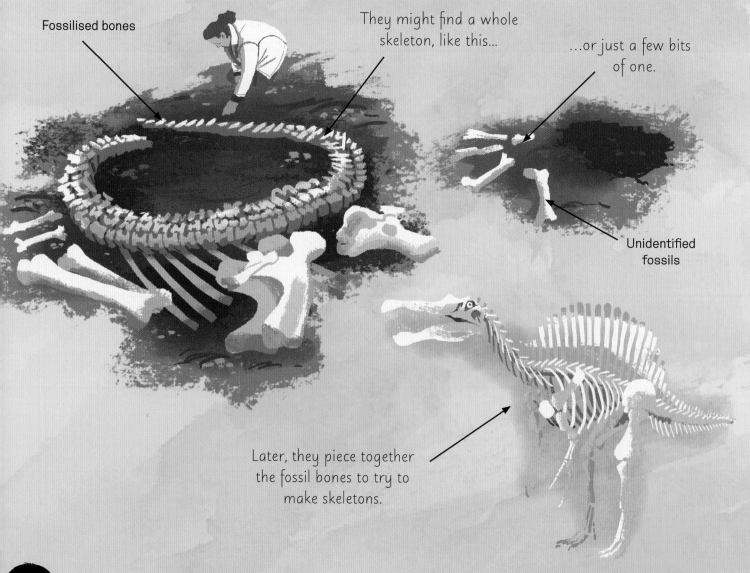

Palaeontologists study fossils and prehistoric life. At a fossil dig, they uncover fossils and carefully take them out of the ground.

They carefully clean the rock and dirt away from each fossil.

Fossilised bones

They might find a whole skeleton, like this...

...or just a few bits of one.

Unidentified fossils

Later, they piece together the fossil bones to try to make skeletons.

PALAEONTOLOGY PUZZLES

When there are only a few bones, it's hard to tell what the rest of the animal looked like - so palaeontologists have to make guesses based on clues.

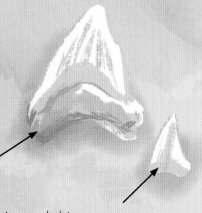

This giant shark tooth fossil was found in Peru.

It's much bigger than a great white shark tooth.

From this, we know that a giant shark must have existed. It's known as megalodon.

HUMAN BONES

Fossilised human bones, and old bones found in caves, can tell us a lot about what people were like in the past and how they lived.

Thousands of years ago, other species of human existed. They had different skulls and skeletons to modern humans.

Flores human
(*Homo floresiensis*)
was much shorter than us.

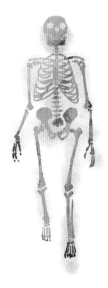

Neanderthal
(*Homo neanderthalensis*)
had a bigger skull than us.

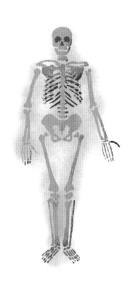

Modern human
(*Homo sapiens*)

GLOSSARY

Archeologist
Someone who studies human bones and old objects to find out about the past.

Bone marrow
Soft substance found inside bones, where blood cells are made.

Calcium
A mineral found in bones and teeth.

Cartilage
A rubbery, bendy substance similar to bone, found in some animals' skeletons.

Cartilaginous fish
Fish with skeletons made mostly of cartilage, such as sharks and rays.

Casque
A helmet-shaped part of the skeleton, usually found on an animal's head.

Compact bone
A strong, solid type of bone.

Crest
A ridged or pointed part of the skeleton that sticks up from an animal's head or back.

Exoskeleton
A tough outer skin or shell that some animals, such as insects, have instead of bones.

Fenestrae
Natural holes or openings in bones.

Fossil
The remains of dead animals, often their bones, that have been preserved as shapes in rocks.

Invertebrate
An animal without a backbone or spine, or other internal bones.

Ivory
Hard, yellowish-white substance made from teeth, usually the tusks of elephants.

Keel
A blade-like part that sticks out from the sternum of a bird, which its flight muscles attach to.

Mandibles
An animal's jaws or jawbones.

Nocturnal
Active at night instead of during the day.

Operculum
Part of a fish's skeleton that covers the gills.

Opposable thumb
A thumb that is positioned opposite the fingers, giving an animal the ability to hold things easily.

Ossicones
Small bone horns found on the skull of a giraffe.

Osteoderms
Lumps or plates of bone that grow in an animal's skin, and protect it like armour.

Otoliths
Bones in the ear that help with hearing, especially in fish.

Palaeontologist
Someone who studies prehistoric life, often by looking at fossils.

Periosteum
The tough outer covering of a bone.

Phalanges
Toe and finger bones.

Plastron
Part of the skeleton of a tortoise or turtle, forming a shell that protects its underside.

Prehistoric
Dating from before humans began making written records of events.

Sclerotic rings
Rings of bone found around the eye sockets in the skeletons of many animals.

Scutes
Plates of a fingernail-like material that make up the shell of a tortoise or turtle.

Spongy bone
A type of hard bone with spaces inside, giving it a sponge-like appearance.

Sternum
A bone in the front of an animal's chest that connects to the ribs and holds them together.

Tailbone
A series of small bones at the lower end of the spine, found in some animals, such as humans and chimps, instead of a tail.

Tendons
Strong, flexible cords that attach muscles to bones.

Urostyle
A long bone at the lower end of the spine, found in frogs and toads.

Vertebrate
An animal that has a backbone or spine, along with other internal bones.